The Family Farm Crisis

Solution!

By Glenn Sellnow

This book is dedicated to my late father Harley Sellnow. He started dairy farming using work horses instead of tractors and lived his full life working on a farm. He died peacefully sitting in the shade of a giant 100 year old apple tree on the same farm where he was born. The apple tree was unsafe because it had been internally hollowed out by large black ants and yet my father would not give permission to have it cut down. It still produced a good amount of green summer apples which he enjoyed eating while sitting in its shade in spite of the danger of it falling down. He said that the tree could be cut down only after he died.

My friend Toan from Viet Nam once observed my father cleaning out our barn which lacked a mechanical chain barn cleaner and said that our farm was more primitive than Viet Nam and he wondered why we would continue to live on the farm. My father had already advised me to leave the farm after I completed high school. He said there was no money to be made there and I should instead go someplace where I could make a profit. That advice seemed to work for me but I am still a farm boy at heart.

Copyright

Table of Contents

Disclaimer

Although the author and publisher have made every effort to ensure that the information in this book was correct at press time, the author and publisher do not assume and hereby disclaim any liability to any party for any loss, damage, or disruption caused by errors or omissions, whether such errors or omissions result from negligence, accident, or any other cause.

This book describes my own personal experiences. I have tried to recreate events, locales and conversations from my memories of them. In order to maintain their anonymity in some instances I have changed the names of individuals and places, I may have changed some identifying characteristics and details such as physical properties, occupations and places of residence. Some of the material in this book may also be available in my blog postings. No organization or individual has endorsed the ideas presented in this book.

I am not a doctor and you should always consult a doctor about anything related to medicine or your health before any action is taken. This book is not intended as a substitute for the medical advice of physicians. The reader should regularly consult a physician in matters relating to his/her health and particularly with respect to any symptoms that may require diagnosis or medical attention. I do not assume any liability for the use or misuse of the ideas contained in this book.

Some quotes from the Bible in this book may be from the KJV translation. The KJV may not follow the latest social fads in the english language but it works for me and most people can understand what it means. Other translations of the Bible may be just as reliable. I have not studied the original Hebrew, Greek and Aramaic text. This makes me a weak Biblical scholar so take everything I say with a grain of salt and consult your local clergy with any questions.

No religious group endorses anything I write regarding the Bible. The Bible is inerrant in its original language and contains many types of literature which are difficult to interpret along with the simple Gospel that even a child can understand. My hope is that I have not misinterpreted any Biblical passage but I can make mistakes because I am only human. If any quotes in this book have been taken out of context in your opinion just contact me at

www.glennsellnow.wordpress.com and I will take the

appropriate corrective action.

About the Author

The short story is that I grew up on a Dairy farm in

Wisconsin, became a professional engineer and married a

hot Sicilian babe from Milwaukee. My name is written in the

Lamb's Book of Life and I was Time Magazine's 2006

"Person of the Year". My cat loves me. I have cancer that

can't be removed surgically and other severe medical conditions but I am making my best effort to survive these issues and die of extreme old age.

I am an imperfect Christian, married with two children and a former Professional Engineer . Traveled around the United States and Canada for engineering work at dairy plants and pharmaceuticals. Grew up on a dairy farm with a large garden and fruit trees. I am a farm boy at heart trapped in the city by circumstance. I have Cancer, Crohn's disease and other serious illness but I am not quite dead just yet.

I like Gardening, Glass Bottle Crafts, Science, Johnny Cash, Animals of all types, Collecting tools, Packers Football and spending time with my family sometimes. I dislike riding in small planes, Cancer, filling out bureaucratic forms and busybodies. I would be quite happy if I never had to travel again anywhere for any reason.

Graduated from Milwaukee School of Engineering. Worked

at the Sellnow Dairy farm, Wurtz Specialty Ice, Lindberg

Industrial Furnaces/Ovens, APV Crepaco

(Dairy/Food/Nuclear) and Seiberling Associates

(Dairy/Pharmaceutical). The most entertaining engineering

project that I ever worked on was at the Dannon Yogurt

company in Ft. Worth, Texas.

The Farm Crisis

Why do some people hate the small family farm? I have

personally talked to seemingly normal people that want to

see the family farm eliminated from our society because they

dislike the concept. Small and midsize family farms are

being gobbled up by fewer large family farms and a few

large corporate farms according to the USDA . [1] " Large

---

[1] Large Family Farms Continue To Dominate US Agricultural Production

corporations play an important role in setting procurement standards and organizing supply chains for farm products, but they directly operate very few U.S. farms."[2] Large family farms are better than corporate farm but I believe there are solutions to saving the small family farm and even creating microfarms in urban areas. A desirable way of life is currently disappearing along with the economic and social benefits that way of life provides our society. This drain on the number of small farms should be stopped and then reversed for the good of our country.

United States farmers have a healthy attitude towards hard work that the rest of the people in the USA could really use to improve our society. Farmers generally have faith in God and good family values which are desirable qualities for any society. Large corporate farms with remote managers may not develop these qualities easily. What most farmers do not have is the benefit of well thought out government

---

[2] https://www.ers.usda.gov/amber-waves/2017/march/large-family-farms-continue-to-dominate-us-agricultural-production/

policies, effective lobbyists in Congress, control over the prices of their products, direct access to consumers or the ability to mitigate their production costs easily. Not all small farmers have been eliminated yet and I believe it is a mistake to allow the elimination of the small family farm from our country. The solutions to stop the loss of family farms must be multifaceted to succeed. Small farmers must have a flexible attitude, a strong cooperative government lobby to change policy, the ability to sell some types of product directly to the public, diversified products and develop a sympathetic public to help them function efficiently.

Examples from other countries farmers may be useful to integrate into the unique american farmer action plan for increased profit. Successful farming operations in European countries could be copied or modified to fit into an American profit structure. Europe has a larger number of small farms versus large farms than the United States but still has economically successful farms in many cases. [3] Why is that true and how do the European small farms survive so easily? We also need to remember the lessons from the extinct Soviet Union and from countries like North Korea to see what happens when the small farm controlled by a generational resident family is eliminated from society.

Large corporate farms with owners not living on the farm are not the smartest idea in the world. Fortunately this is only a fraction of the number of farms that exist today. Good efficiency on a large or small farm can only be achieved by continuous generational resident family ownership in my opinion. This book will demonstrate why a larger number of small family farms would benefit our society.and will present solutions on how to achieve this worthwhile goal.

3

https://www.ers.usda.gov/webdocs/publications/40408/30642_wrs0404b_002.pdf?v=0

Prejudice and Ignorance

Popular media has cast somewhat negative stereotypes on American farmers over the years. Farmers used to be portrayed in the media as simple country bumpkins living in poverty and having poor clothing. Now they are shown as greedy corporate farmers abusing their animals, poisoning the soil and causing global climate change. People ignorant of farm reality don't really care enough to learn the truth about farms because it doesn't directly impact their lives. There are savvy anti-farm groups using the media that are only too happy to exploit these stereotypes. The total ignorance of food production and farming techniques in the general population is frightening and dangerous for electing

congressional representatives that do what their constituents

want them to do.

PETA is one organization that is not friendly to the American

farmer. Dairy farms are only one of their targets. "Aside

from "lactose-tolerant" white supremacists, cow's milk really

is the perfect drink of choice for *all* (even unwitting)

supremacists, since the dairy industry inflicts extreme

violence on other living beings. PETA is trying to wake

people up to the implications of choosing this white beverage

and suggesting that they choose something else pronto."[4]

This statement in PETA literature is so obviously a bunch of

cow manure that it is a shame it needs to be discussed by

reasonable people. The attitude of the PETA propaganda

machine is dangerous because it could infect the

educational system and produce prejudice against farmers in

---

[4] https://www.peta.org/blog/cows-milk-perfect-drink-supremacists/

children. This type of hate speech against farmers needs to be rejected by all elements of our society. Perhaps lawsuits by farmers organization would be appropriate for some types of anti-farmer hate speech propaganda. It is probably more effective to spend effort on positive actions rather than trying to correct the statements of radical haters.

One of the latest anti-farmer concepts is that emissions from American cows are causing global climate change so dairy farming should be eliminated. Let's think about this with some historical perspective. The United States used to have vast herds of bison that turned the horizon black with their numbers until we butchered them in mass for their pelts and let their carcasses rot. Didn't bison emit a little gas while they were alive? It is ridiculous to promote the elimination of dairy farming to prevent climate change because of cow gas. All types of cattle can eat a diet that is high in alfalfa, grasses and some types of agricultural by products. All of these cattle food sources are ecologically sound for the environment. Grasses can be harvested without disturbing the soil every year as is needed for other crops. Grass can also be grown in poor soil conditions that would not directly support food crops for human consumption. Recycling agricultural by-products such as large amounts of future hemp waste for cattle feed is so sensible that no one should be opposed to it. Additionally some types of cattle can graze directly on land that would otherwise be useless for agricultural purposes.

Society Benefits from Small Family Farms

Small business of any type creates jobs and farms are

always capable of producing plenty of work. The issue is

that everyone gets paid but the farmer for the value he

provides society. The more farms you have the more

society benefits economically. "In 2017, 21.6 million full- and

part-time jobs were related to the agricultural and food

sectors—11.0 percent of total U.S. employment. Direct on-farm employment accounted for about 2.6 million of these jobs, or 1.3 percent of U.S. employment. Employment in agriculture- and food-related industries supported another 19.0 million jobs. Of this, food service, eating and drinking places accounted for the largest share—12.5 million jobs— and food/beverage stores supported 3.2 million jobs. The remaining agriculture-related industries together added another 3.3 million jobs."[5]

Farmers have the right attitude for America. Farmers are the type of people that produce something society really needs in an efficient manner. I have seen a great number of people in other careers that produce things that ruin our society and manage to put a drain on our economy at the same time. Politicians are a prime example that spring into my mind. Fortunately, farmers and people living in rural states have a disproportionate positive effect on the makeup of our national politicians due to the wisdom of our founding

---

[5] https://www.ers.usda.gov/data-products/ag-and-food-statistics-charting-the-essentials/ag-and-food-sectors-and-the-economy/

fathers. The "Tyranny of the Majority" is difficult to achieve in the United States because the electoral college elects the President and the number of Senators per state is not based on population of the individual state. The electoral college gives more weight to rural states which gives farmers a greater voice in politics if they are organized during elections. The makeup of the House of Representatives is directly based on population and it shows up in House proposed government policies that are anti-farmer. The vast bulk of people in states with less farmers have little knowledge regarding the reality of producing their food. Compromise is needed to get anything done because people in rural states tend to have different values than people living in the major population centers without a lot of farmers. The founding fathers of our country knew exactly what they were doing when they designed the structure of the electoral college and Senate. Of course that's natural because many of them were farmers.

Government Policy Changes Are Needed

It should be legal to sell raw and processed milk products directly to the end consumer from the farm where it is produced as long at is clearly labeled with handling instructions. Consumers want to buy raw milk and will pay dairy farmers real cash money at a good price for these types of dairy products. I personally know rich consumers that drive over an hour just to buy their raw milk from a farmer because they believe it provides health benefits. Milk from cows, goats and more exotic mammals could also be included to provide novel interest to the consumer and help consumers that can't digest normal pasteurized cow milk. I know of at least one fairly large dairy farming operation in Wisconsin that has dairy cows and dairy goats on the same farm in a successful business model. Farmers should be able to set their own price for milk products sold on their farm.

"Raw milk is directly sold to customers at farms in countries such as France, Germany, Denmark, Italy, the Netherlands, Czech Republic, Austria, Slovakia, Lithuania, Ireland and the U.K.

They found many dairy farmers produce traditional cheese, buttermilk, yogurt and chocolate from raw milk in their farms. The major countries that have adopted raw milk vending machines include Italy, France, Romania, Germany, the U.K., Slovakia, Slovenia and Czech Republic.

According to ReportLinker, the key reason for adoption of raw milk vending machine was due to the revisions in regulations of respective countries regarding raw milk sales. Furthermore, the majority of end-users in these countries prefer drinking raw milk and consuming raw milk related products due to their nutritional benefits."[6]

My entire family while I was a child drank fresh raw milk from our farm and ate a diet including lots of quality cheese from the Widmer's cheese company.. Farmers need to cut out the middleman and sell raw milk directly to the consumer for the purpose of making more profit like they do in Europe. Let the small dairy farmer make the profit that is currently being made by the milk processor on some percentage of his milk production. Consumers are willing to pay exorbitant prices for raw milk from cows and goats.

---

[6] https://www.foodsafetynews.com/2017/03/europes-raw-milk-vending-machines-come-in-for-market-scrutiny/

It may even be possible for small farmers to make deals with high quality cheese plants to sell the processors quality cheese or similar products in an adjacent vending machine for a cut of the profit. Deals could be made with other types of product providers to sell their products on the farm and an entire farm experience could also be sold as a destination experience. Hayrides, corn mazes, Halloween pumpkin patches, Self picking fruit, Milking a cow, driving an old tractor or observing the birth of a calf could be incorporated into a business model for a small farm of this nature if practical for the location and if desired by the farmer. I have seen some small farms in Wisconsin doing this to generate extra income.

Reasonably priced health insurance should be made available to farmers and all citizens of the United States by law. I know of farmers who have lost their business because a family member became ill and the money was sucked out of their farm to pay for medical bills. My mother was unable to obtain insurance at any reasonable price because she had a preexisting condition. Some socialist type government policies like they have in Europe are needed in the United States to insure there is an adequate safety net like President Ronald Reagan talked about.

The idea that you will be financially ruined and lose your farm or business due to illness while you are a citizen of an advanced rich country like the USA is stupid. Farmers in Japan are not financially ruined by an illness because there is a national health care plan in Japan that is run efficiently. We actually bombed Japan with atomic weapons and leveled entire cities in Germany to the ground. Now all of their people have better healthcare than we do along with a higher standard of living with a capitalist economy. I am not a big fan of the Obamacare implementation but health care should be reformed at the national level by politicians that do not have San Francisco values. Every citizen of the USA should have optional access to a national healthcare plan that is similar to the Japanese and German examples. The USA can do it if Japan and Germany can do it.

Tariffs should be imposed on any country that does not allow our agricultural products to be imported in a fair manner. I am not a big fan of everything President Trump has done but President Trump was right to level the import/export playing field with other countries by the use of tariffs as a negotiation tactic. Unfair competition with other countries has been tolerated in the past but we need to be more vigilant and we should be willing to threaten and impose the same tariffs that other countries impose on our agricultural products.

We need to export more beef to Japan. "TOKYO -- Japan is becoming a nation of carnivores, as consumption of beef and other types of meat continues to rise amid changing lifestyles. Japanese today eat nearly 20% more meat per person than they did just two decades ago ...Japan's livestock industry policy has so far largely focused on protecting domestic producers as imports have expanded. But unless the policy shifts to enhancing the industry's competitiveness, there may be a backlash from consumers over supply shortages or higher prices."[7] Japanese are currently paying outrageous prices for beef by american standards because the Japanese government is protecting their domestic producers but the Japanese people are insisting they still want good old red meat even at high prices. American farmers can fill that order if our government would negotiate a fair deal on importing beef to Japan.

When I was in the FFA back in Lomira my project was to raise a purebred Holstein milking cow on a share basis for sale at the Dodge county fair. I was fortunate enough to receive a calf from a farmer for this project by random

---

[7] https://asia.nikkei.com/Economy/Japan-is-hungry-for-meat-but-domestic-producers-aren-t-feasting

chance that had outstanding genetic ancestry. The animal was so good that someone from Japan bought the Holstein and flew it back to Japan.The average size farm in Japan is just three acres but they still make a profit per acre due to their governments agricultural policies. I bet that cow had a better life in Japan than it would have had living in the United States. That rotten cow nearly killed me once and it attempted to jump off the ramp when it was at the Dodge county fair but it did pay for my first year of college expenses. The Japanese are willing to pay with good green American dollars for higher quality agricultural products.like animals with superior genetics.

Our government needs to open up the Japanese market to our farmers products on a more equitable basis. The government of Japan and its people have implemented agricultural policies that support the small Japanese family farm to the point of absurdity. The United States needs to examine its policies and compare them to the Japanese model for the purpose of promoting high quality American ag products that can command a premium price. Small farms require a high profit ratio per acre to support a family and increased agricultural exports should tend to increase the price that farmers are paid for their crops and products..

Tax policies and zoning rules should be changed to favor the continuation and expansion of the number of small family farms. Intensive agriculture on small farms similar to the Japanese model should be completely tax exempt, have farm friendly zoning ordinances and right to farm laws even if the farmer has a second job. Urban agriculture models such as Will Allen's Growing Power in Milwaukee should be encouraged by government grants and public sentiment to continue for the benefit of the community even after the founder retires. I remember a Mong family bought the tiny shell of a farm next to my father's farm and raised vegetables in an intensive manner for a good profit. Small farms producing high value nontraditional or experimental crops should be exempt from taxes and be encouraged by the government in every possible way.

To the best of my knowledge the Mong family have since moved on to bigger and better projects however their example should be encouraged by federal and local government. Intensive agriculture that makes more profit per acre should be a natural for increasing the number of small family farms especially for new immigrant farmers willing to work. . Some types of intensive farming require labor that most unfit or lazy americans are simply unwilling to do. Large scale intensive farming requires a lot of labor that is currently being met in a big way by immigrants who perform difficult labor for low pay. I suggest that aging farmers on small farms without heirs should be given government incentive in the form of tax breaks or outright subsidies if they develop a plan to sell their farms to apprentices willing to make a 12 year commitment to work with the existing owner to farm the land and live on it.

Existing American citizens should be given strong economic incentives to undergo this program but immigrants should be considered if they are willing to become American citizens and complete the program. Immigrants from many different countries would jump at a chance for an apprenticeship type farming program in the United States that would eventually make them property owners and create real wealth for them. Priority in access to such a program should be based on capabilities and merit. Large Tech companies import workers from other countries if no american can get the job done so why not give farmers the same opportunity along with taxpayer dollars to encourage the continuation of the small family farm..

Unrestricted hemp production should be nationally legalized as soon as possible to override any type of silly individual state restrictions. "It can be refined into a variety of commercial items, including paper, textiles, clothing, biodegradable

plastics, paint, insulation, biofuel, food, and animal feed." [8]

"The world-leading producer of hemp is China, which produces

more than 70% of the world output."[9] Hemp would eventually

change our industry, agriculture and fuel supply if we just wised

up a little like the people who control the agriculture in China.

Our country could reduce our need for petroleum and other

foreign products while helping the USA become more self

sufficient simultaneously..

Large amounts of farmland producing hemp could not be

used for other agricultural products so the law of supply and

demand would force up the price of other ag products to the

benefit of all farmers of any type. Dairy farmers for instance

would have the option of reducing crop production needed

for cow feed and adding crop land for more profitable hemp

production. Milk production would decrease and the supply

of milk would be reduced. The price of Dairy products would

---

[8] https://en.wikipedia.org/wiki/Hemp
[9] https://en.wikipedia.org/wiki/Hemp

rise until an equilibrium is reached between milk and hemp. A large scale hemp based economy would help all american farmers by raising the price of their existing products and giving them the alternative option of producing some hemp. Hemp production is probably more suited to midsize and large scale farming operations but it should improve the prices for small farm products by removing competition from larger farms for the same product in a saturated market.

Organic and GMO food from large producers should be labeled clearly as to what is in the food like the labeling requirements in Europe. The European Union makes it difficult for american GMO food products to enter their countries because GMO products can only be sold after being scientifically authorised by European Union experts. This helps to protect their farmers from American competition. GMO foods should be clearly labeled as GENETICALLY MODIFIED ORGANISM in big letters because people have a right to know what they put in their bodies. Foods using non-organic pesticides and herbicides should be clearly labeled with large labels. Organic and nonGMO crops are typically produced on smaller farms near the point at which they are sold and require more labor intensive practices to produce. This would create more jobs and would probably result in the consumer choosing more organic foods and thereby funding and encouraging more small farms. The European Union's restrictive labeling laws involving GMOs and pesticide tainted products may be one of the reasons they have more small farms with a better profit ratio.

Organically grown marijuanna should be legalized just like cigarettes and alcohol. It is a high profit cash crop that is against the law in some states due to legal prohibition. The United States tried to outlaw alcohol and failed. Prohibiting adults from using marijuanna does not seem to be an effective way to use the time of our law enforcement officers because prohibition does not work in the United States as proven by the experiment with prohibiting alcohol. Farmers should be allowed to process and sell marijuanna, alcohol and tobacco directly from their farms along with other farm products rather than restricting distribution channels to middle men under corporate or government control.

I would never personally use pot unless a doctor prescribed it for some illness however prohibition is a diversion of needed government resources because pot consumption is not being stopped by police action. It should not be legally treated different than alcohol and cigarettes because people have moral objections to all three products. Small farms are well suited to growing and selling marijuanna for profit. Small illegal farms are making a profit right now so legalization would only improve these types of profit. The legal production and sale of marijuanna would reduce the production of other types of agricultural produce because land would be used for pot instead of other crops. This would drive up the price of all ag products to the benefit of all farmers.

I know I may receive some flak from my conservative friends for supporting the total legalization of marijuanna for adults but it should be legally compared to cigarettes and alcohol in my opinion. Everyone can agree agree that cigarettes and alcohol kill people right now. What could be worse? Yet they are legal but pot is not? That is simply unreasonable and everyone knows that selective prohibition does not make logical sense.. All three would be eliminated in a perfect world but this is not a perfect world.

It is the business of government to manage the imperfections in this world in a consistent and logical manner. The war against pot has already failed so we might as well allow farmers to make a profit from it rather than allowing criminal drug lords to rake in the money and kill people with thugs to protect their illegal business. The money used in the failed attempt to police pot would be

better spent on promoting american ag products in

appropriate foreign markets.

Medical Marijuanna prescribed and monitored by a doctor for

real diseases should definitely be allowed. I have Crohn's

disease and a scientific study done in Israel indicate that

marijuanna could be used to treat crohn's disease. I have

never used marijuanna and it would not be my first choice for

treatment. "Although the primary end point of the study

(induction of remission) was not achieved, a short course (8

weeks) of THC-rich cannabis produced significant clinical,

steroid-free benefits to 10 of the 11 patients with active

Crohn's disease, compared with placebo, without side

effects. Further studies, with larger patient groups and a

nonsmoking mode of intake, are warranted.

ClinicalTrials.gov, NCT01040910."[10]

---

[10] https://www.ncbi.nlm.nih.gov/pubmed/23648372

In my best estimate legal marijuanna will cause people to die and ruin the lives of many just like legal cigarettes and legal alcohol are currently doing. I find it difficult to believe that legal marijuanna will make our society worse than the problems we already have with prohibition of marijuana. Prohibition of marijuanna does not seem to have stopped people from using it but criminals are becoming rich and government resources are being diverted from other more urgent needs to fight a hopeless war on prohibited marijuanna consumption and production. What good does this secular prohibition do? Save the taxpayer money and let the Church work to save the souls and attitudes of those who abuse any drug. Knowingly distributing any illegal substance to a minor should receive severe penalties such as a fine based on a significant percentage of your legal income for 18 years plus other penalties as decided by the courts.

Governments have a poor track record at succeeding in changing people's morals and saving their souls from their own vices The most effective thing the government can do is to severely attack the profits by high taxation or income proportional fines of anyone distributing cigarettes, alcohol, marijuana or any type of undesirable substances to minors. Adults should know better and are free to make their own decisions. Adults using undesirable substances might as well help alleviate the farm crisis with their cash rather than giving that cash to violent drug lords that don't give a damn about our society.

Farmers need high value crops and there may be other potential options that will produce the same high profit ratio as marijuana, alcohol and tobacco. All plants with potentially positive pharmaceutical value need to be considered for future farm crops and the government should pay farmers for growing research crops in this arena just like it pays doctors to research other new medicines..Plants of this nature can be marketed as a cheaper natural option rather than using

harsh artificial drugs. Pharmaceutical companies will fight

this concept because they will lose profit on their drugs

which may have side effects. I think that it's a step in the

right direction for family farms to gain profit at the expense of

giant pharmaceutical companies.

Examples From Other Countries

North Korea has a lot of starving people and South Korea

has abundant food. Why is that true? Could one reason be

that North Korea has collective farm ownership and control.?

South Korea has many small family farms. Which Korea would you want to live in and which country should the United States try to copy?

The old Soviet Union attempted to get rid of the small family farm and establish communist collective farms. How did that work out for them? Not that well. The leaders of the now extinct U.S.S.R. eventually decide to change this mistaken policy because they discovered that people simply stop working or didn't work that hard because they did not profit from the crop on a collective farm. The leaders decided to give out individual plots of land like in a capitalist economy and allow the small farmers to profit from their work.

"Although accounting for a small share of cultivated area, private plots produced a substantial share of the country's meat, milk, eggs, and vegetables.[citation needed] Although never more than 4% of the arable land in the USSR, private plots consistently yielded a quarter to a third of total produce. In other words, private plots were more than 8 to 12 times as productive. Private plots were among many attempts made to restructure Soviet farming.[citation needed] However, the weak worker incentives and managerial autonomy, which were the crux of the problem, were not addressed.[citation needed]

The private plots were also an important source of income for rural households. In 1977, families of kolkhoz members obtained 72% of their meat, 76% of their eggs and most of their potatoes from private holdings. Surplus products, as well as surplus livestock, were sold to *kolkhozy* and *sovkhozy* and also to state consumer cooperatives. Statistics may actually under-represent the total contribution of private plots to Soviet agriculture.[14] The only time when private plots were completely banned was during collectivization, when famine took millions of lives.[15]

Capitalism clearly is more efficient at producing food from farming than Communism. Although the Soviet Union was the world's second leading agricultural producer and ranked first in the production of numerous commodities, agriculture was a net drain on the economy." [11]

---

[11] https://en.wikipedia.org/wiki/Agriculture_in_the_Soviet_Union

Action Plan for Farmers

"And he said, The things which are impossible with men are

possible with God."

Luke 18:27, NIV

Farmers need to avoid always looking at situations as just a

problem and instead always think of everything as an

opportunity to make a profit. Global climate change should

be a great marketing gimmick for farm products from small

local farms if they get the proper marketing support from politicians. Local farms that sell directly to consumers save the environment by reducing the amount of fossil fuels needed for transportation and produce a renewable resource. Farmers should make sure the politicians they elect promote a positive image of small local farms to the general public. The opinion of the general public is important to create demand for specific American farm products.

Farmers should stop giving away everything for free. Composted animal manure can be sold for a profit and used as a safe soil enhancer for gardeners or anyone growing plants. Purple Cow Organics is one example of a Wisconsin company that sells composted cow manure to the public for a profit. Why should our society use poisonous fertilizers made from irreplaceable fossil fuels that cause climate change when we have plenty of manure to compost and sell. Farmers should follow Purple Cow Organics good example and sell composted manure directly from the farm or in distributing stores while advertising all products sold on their farm to the public. Laws could be passed that tax non-organic fertilizers based on nonrenewable petroleum for the purpose of making safe organic composted cow manure more economically attractive to the end consumer. Of course recycling cow manure for fertilizer helps the consumer fight global climate change by reducing their carbon footprint. My father would have gotten quite a laugh out of selling composted manure directly to consumers. I find this concept amusing myself but it is a viable business model for a processed organic product.

Farmers need to politically organize to maximize their impact on the choice of political representation, especially at the national level. Farmers need to Insist that all politicians from farm states vote for immediate total hemp deregulation and conversion to a hemp biofuel economy for the purpose of powering most transportation systems such as cars. Hemp biofuel will increase farm profits for all farm crops because hemp production will consume a lot of production land and take away production of crops for saturated markets. Biofuel should be marketed as a more green alternative to nonrenewable petroleum that will give the United States total energy independence. Hemp converts sunlight to usable biomass which is the most efficient form of environmental sound solar power for transportation on earth. Even most current electric cars run on electricity generated by dirty coal plants or dangerous atomic energy. Wind power supplies only a small fraction of our electricity and wind turbines require constant replacement and maintenance. Safe clean renewable hemp biofuel is the obvious choice. Farmers may want to hire Greta as a spokesperson in the future.

Almond "milk" has been able to increase its popularity at the expense of real Dairy milk by advertising its environmental and health advantages. Its sad that two different types of farmers have to compete in this manner for shrinking public demand. Dairy farmers are usually local suppliers and could argue that their product is better for the environment because it uses less fossil fuel to transport it. Dairy cattle also can make use of some recycled agricultural waste products such as from industrial hemp which could be a selling point to the environmentally sensitive consumer in the future. Politicians are usually fairly useless scumbags but I believe that farmers should actively try to put them to work promoting their states ag products and trying to increase demand for ag products. Politicians that do things like discouraging children in school from consuming a perfectly healthy product such as milk need to be vigorously opposed by all farmers on moral grounds even if the farmers live in California.

Most farmers should attempt to diversify the types of crops and products they are producing. Diversification makes any business resistant to economic change and upheaval. Industrial hemp is an obvious future cash crop for average size and large farms that would be available to farmers as one option after asinine government controls on hemp are finally totally eliminated. China is currently the leading producer of hemp and produces 70 percent of the world hemp supply. The USA is behind China in hemp production but that needs to change as soon as possible. A future large scale hemp based economy for fuel, plastic substitutes and animal feeds would drive farm prices on other products higher because there would be less of the other products produced. Congress should be told to lift all restrictions on hemp production because it is a renewable resource that will help stop global warming. Growing hemp is good for the environment and so are biodegradable hemp products. High profit per acre crops are needed for all farms in the United States just like farms in Japan and Europe to insure survival of the family farm.

Any product such as raw milk that can be sold directly to consumers on the farm for high profit like they do in Europe should be utilized if the farm location is close to population centers. This allows farmers to cut out the middleman and keep those profits on the farm. Congress should immediately authorize the safe regulated sale of raw milk at farms using vending machines just like most modern European countries already allow.

Farmers should actively support and campaign for politicians that are advocating policies that will help them. Farmers and people in rural areas are positively weighted in the Presidential elections due to the electoral college rules and in the way the Senate is elected. This provides them with a built in national political advantage in the Senate and the Presidency that should be actively exploited to their economic advantage. Rural states such as Iowa are early in the presidential primary race and therefore farmers should use this advantage to help weed out candidates with anti-farmer agendas. The immediate total legalization and exploitation of industrial hemp should be on the agenda for every farmer and elected politicians. Hate speech denigrating normal farm practices should be spoken against by elected politicians and groups doing the hate speech should be socially ostracized. Unfair trade deals with other countries need to be terminated and replaced with fair deals.

Unnatural non organic meat grown in petri type dishes using chemical and genetic manipulation is an industry in its infancy and real farmers should take political and social action to make sure it dies an early death. It represents future competition to natural animal farmers that makes the United States dependent on a food source that is not natural and requires a lot of fragile technological support systems that may not always be available in difficult times. I have nothing against vegans and vegetarians but you need some type of animal products to receive proper nutrients. Nothing is better than a nice natural red meat steak to get those nutrients. Unnatural artificial meat should be clearly labeled as artificial and inorganic to insure consumers know what they are eating.

Consumers like to buy and are willing to pay extra for organic food and organic food is more difficult to raise on large factory farms. Non-organic food should be required by national law to clearly state in large bold letters that it may be contaminated with pesticides, herbicides or Genetically Modified Organisms. Smaller local organic farms would become more numerous with this type of ordinance due to the law of supply and demand. Our society is becoming more health conscience and farmers need to adapt their products to show how healthy and environmentally friendly farm products are.to the public.

Small farms and microfarms need to develop high value per acre crops like Japanese farmers. Selling directly to the public and taking all the profit is especially useful for microfarms. Microfarms and small farms are probably going to require some type of nonfarm income to support a significant size family in the United States for the foreseeable future unless an Amish model of farm community is used. Amish small farms seem to be quite profitable with no difficulty and some aspects of Amish farm business practices could be incorporated into modern microfarms.

I was intrigued with the idea of selling small landscape starter plants from micro farms or backyard nurseries that I saw on Mike McGroaty's website https://mikesbackyardnursery.com/about/ . He has a network of growers and was on the cover of Mother Earth News Magazine. His concepts could also be upscaled and sold to the public as a way to combat global climate change because woody plants sequester carbon from the atmosphere. Landscape plants also incidentally look pretty so it is a win-win scenario for everyone. This idea could also be combined with the edible landscaping movement by selling edible fruit producing plants for the home. There is not any reason that all sizes of farms could not incorporate these ideas as a side crop for profit.

Specialty crops as a farm side business or main business are already encouraged by the government. Grants from the government for the development of these crops should be sought out and incorporated into a farm plan if appropriate to the situation. "A federal grant program offered by USDA's Agricultural Marketing Service, the purpose of the Specialty Crop Multi-State Program is to competitively award funds to projects that enhance the competitiveness of specialty crops by funding collaborative, multi-state projects that address regional or national level specialty crop issues, including food safety, plant pests and disease, research; crop-specific projects addressing common issues; and marketing and promotion.

Specialty crops include fruits and vegetables, tree nuts, dried fruits, horticulture, and nursery crops (including floriculture)."[12] Even if money is from the government it is still useful and should not be looked at in a negative light.

Holland makes an economically profitable national business out of tulips and other flowers. Cranberries, Almonds and nursery crops are good money makers. Why should the average farmer be losing money on the same old crops when the government will pay the farmer to develop new high value crops. I wouldn't bet the farm on a specialty crop because failure is possible but I would be willing to risk taxpayer dollars to help me develop a side crop with the potential for high profit per acre if I was a farmer. Any size farm should have the right

[12] https://datcp.wi.gov/Pages/Growing_WI/SpecialtyCrops.aspx

to apply for these grants and the pay off may be significant even for micro farms along the Japanese farm model. Door county farms in Wisconsin have specialty wines and native fruits such as gooseberries which are good examples of what a small farm can produce for a high profit ratio per acre.

Growing some types of currently existing labor intensive high profit vegetables in climate controlled factories instead may prove profitable in the future and is currently in the profitable experimental stage. Northern farmers may want to look at adding some cash crop production capability of this type to their farms as the techniques become more developed. Development can be subsidized by the government or corporation partners can simply take care of the initial capital investment for the purpose of sharing the long term profits. California currently produces a lot of expensive vegetables year round but it has water shortages and strangling government regulations that do not exist in other states.

Honey is an excellent side crop/product for small local farms and honeybees are not doing that well. Honeybees are needed for many types of crops and the survival of humans on earth. Government grants should be made available to subsidize any farm willing to work with honey. Local honey is an excellent product to sell directly from a small farm because it has medical benefits for some people and it tastes great. Best of all the bees do most of the work. Honey Acres in Wisconsin is one such excellent company that also gives out tours of their facility.

The need to maintain genetic diversity in our plant and animals is not a bad idea. Large monoculture agriculture enterprises are vulnerable to the rapid spread of disease in plants and animals. The human race can't anticipate which types of genetic material will be useful for survival in the event of severe climate change, environmental changes or a new disease spreading across the globe. I just saw on television news that a new deadly mystery disease originating in China is affecting both humans and animals (01/18/2020). Saving animals and plants from extinction will make sure that their unique genetic code is available to combat changing requirements such as resistance to the potato blight which caused starvation in Ireland during 1845.

The government should pay farmers to maintain diverse genetic stock of noncommercial animals and plants that may not be commercially viable at this time but may be critical to human survival in the future. Small farms are ideal for this purpose and it would provide these farms with a guaranteed income. Animals being raised for this purpose could also be shown to the public for educational purposes and on a paid basis for a zoo type experience. The Milwaukee Public Zoo has a small animal farm type of experience and petting zoo of this nature but why can't farmers collect some money from the government while expanding on the zoo model?

The Vikings established a Greenland colony in the 10th century beginning with the voyage of Erik the Red in 985. Climate change may have been one factor affecting the end of their colony although there may have been related factors. The Little Ice Age was taking place in Europe and North America at this time and it was affecting agricultural production and the types of plants that would grow well. Earth's climate is clearly not stable and it does change even without the intervention of human pollution. We know this is true because we have historical evidence in the Little Ice Age between 1300 and 1870 and significant human pollution did not exist in 1300. The Vikings would probably still be in Greenland today if they had just diversified their animals/plants and adopted the sea food gathering methods of the native Inuit. We should learn from the Viking example to be flexible in agriculture and food supply sources to insure our own civilizations survival.

All farmers need more profit per acre farmed regardless of the number of acres on the farm. Higher production is not always equivalent to higher profit especially if the consumer market is saturated due to the law of supply and demand. Japanese farmers have no problem making a profit per acre on farms of 3 acres because they use intensive agriculture to produce a high quality product and are paid a premium price for it. This same concept could be used in the United States in some circumstances. Most Japanese farmers also have other jobs in addition to farming even though their farms make a profit. European farmers have average farm sizes of 39 acres and still make a profit per acre due to government protection, government subsidies, high value products and the nature of their society's opinion about traditional quality products. Some farms in the United States should attempt to copy certain concepts of Japan and Europe to improve

their profit ratio per acre.

A diversified family farm with direct access to

consumer money is more likely to survive over

generations than a monoculture farm without

nonfarm income because the demand for specific

farm products change over long periods of time

affecting profit. Flexibility in crop and animals being

raised along with retail income for value added

products/services are a positive factor in allowing

farms to remain in the same family for generations.

Amish farms in the United States are one example

among others that confirm this fact is accurate.

Good family values and trust in God procure

economic cohesion for generational farm families in

addition to providing a positive lifestyle that affects

the nature of our country.

Small Farms Mitigate National Emergencies

"There was no food, however, in the whole region because the famine was severe; both Egypt and Canaan wasted away because of the famine."

Genesis 47:13 NIV

https://my.bible.com/bible/111/GEN.47.13.NIV

There are several severe national emergency scenarios where it would be useful to have a country wide distributed network of small family farms operating with minimal external input and capable of providing food to people. In many of these situations it may be to the individuals advantage to already be living on a farm and have the ability to survive and help others. I am fairly confident that FEMA has already examined situations that would require its activation and the cooperation of the general population but the government may not have the resources to deal with simultaneous problems in a timely manner.

A fairly recent in my lifetime example of a small single crisis was Hurricane Katrina. "The Louisiana Superdome was opened as a, "refuge of last resort," for those residents that were unable to obtain safe transport out of the city. 20,000 people entered the Dome. The Louisiana National Guard had delivered three truckloads of water and seven truckloads

of MRE's to the Superdome, enough to supply 15,000

people for three days."[13] Obviously this was an insufficient

response to a disaster that was easy to predict in advance.

Severe national emergency scenarios could include natural

disasters and man made mistakes. Disasters could also

include a combination of FEMA mistakes or inadequacy in

response to these situations.

The Solar Storm of 1859 was a real historical event that

didn't do much damage because our economy was not

based on electricity like it is now. This event could easily

happen again within our lifetime. "In June 2013, a joint

venture from researchers at Lloyd's of London and

Atmospheric and Environmental Research (AER) in the

United States used data from the Carrington Event to

estimate the current cost of a similar event to the U.S. alone

at $0.6–2.6 trillion."[14] "One serious threat to the reliability of

---

[13] https://en.wikipedia.org/wiki/Timeline_of_Hurricane_Katrina

electric power is geomagnetic storms – severe disturbances caused by solar storms in the upper layers of our atmosphere that induce currents in long conductors on the Earth's surface, such as power lines. These additional currents can overload the electric grid system to trigger voltage collapse, or worse, damage a significant number of expensive extra-high voltage transformers. The economic costs of such an event would be catastrophic. Large transformer repairs/replacements occur on the timescale of weeks to months, and could result in long-term widespread blackouts."[15] The world could temporarily be without electricity, refrigeration and transportation until the grid can be repaired in several months or longer. Access to food and water could be enhanced during this predictable event if a network of small local farms were available.

---

[14] https://en.wikipedia.org/wiki/Solar_storm_of_1859
[15] Lloyd's and Atmospheric and Environmental Research, Inc. (2013). *Solar storm risk to the north American electric grid* (PDF). With input from Homeier, Nicole; Horne, Richard; Maran, Michael; Wade, David. Lloyd's. Retrieved July 31,2019.

In 1812 the Mississippi river ran backwards due to earthquakes on the New Madrid fault line. This will happen again eventually because fault lines do not magically disappear. "In a report filed in November 2008, the U.S. Federal Emergency Management Agency warned that a serious earthquake in the New Madrid Seismic Zone could result in "the highest economic losses due to a natural disaster in the United States," further predicting "widespread and catastrophic" damage across Alabama, Arkansas, Illinois, Indiana, Kansas, Kentucky, Mississippi, Missouri, Oklahoma, Texas, and particularly Tennessee, where a 7.7 magnitude quake would cause damage to tens of thousands of structures affecting water distribution, transportation systems, and other vital infrastructure.[21] The earthquake is expected to also result in many thousands of fatalities, with more than 4,000 of the fatalities expected in Memphis alone."[16] Transporting food to an area affected by such an earthquake may be difficult when there are no road because

---

[16] https://en.wikipedia.org/wiki/New_Madrid_Seismic_Zone

of earthquake damage. Local access to a renewable food source for a few years would be very handy.

Scientists seem to agree that the Yellowstone Super Volcano is overdue for some type of activity but predicting volcano behaviour may not be the most accurate science in the world. Minor activity would simply be an oddity for tourists but a significant eruption of a supervolcano in the center of the United States could ruin your day at least. A major full scale caldera eruption is capable of ending civilization as we know it and sending the world into a food scarcity condition because of the world wide ash cloud obscuring sunlight needed for agriculture. Farm stockpiles of grain being reserved for animal food or other purposes would suddenly be more valuable as food for starving human beings. Cattle and other animals capable of feeding on existing surviving vegetation and being converted into meat for humans would also be in high demand. Priorities would change quickly in an event of this nature.

In my estimation the Amish community will survive a potential supervolcano major eruption for the long term without too many problems. They have small self sufficient farming communities and are not dependent on the latest technology. Their common faith in God will allow them to function as an economic community when the rest of the people in the technologically dependent world will panic in fear. Some types of vegetation will eventually grow in the reduced light caused by a major ash cloud which can be directly consumed by humans. Other types of vegetation can be converted by cattle and other animals into meat that humans can consume and will provide them with some nutrients that can not be obtained by eating the remaining vegetation by itself. Perhaps the Amish aren't as backwards and quaint as they seem now? It may even be possible that FEMA could learn something from the Amish example before a real major catastrophe occurs.

An asteroid strike resulting in a global dust cloud would be an event that could be treated in a similar manner to a major volcanic eruption. It has happened before and will happen again at some random location on the earth. This is not a high probability event for our life time but I would be willing to bet that someone at FEMA has spent your tax dollars figuring out how to deal with it.. Nuclear war would have similar results except it would be initiated by man's stupidity.

Genetically Modified Organisms seem to be working in an acceptable manner to enhance our current food supply however scientists are capable of making mistakes. One example of a past scientific mistake is the release of killer bees in the western hemisphere during a program designed to breed better bees. GMOs have the potential of crossbreeding with other plants in ways that scientists did not plan. Genetic material inserted in a plant from an unrelated species could spread in the plant world and cause unexpected results that can not be controlled. I consider this a low probability event but it is not completely impossible.

Intelligent terrorists or agents of a government hostile to the United States could deliberately genetically modify plants, animals or related microorganisms to produce an undesirable effect on our food supply or directly on human life that could be difficult to isolate and eliminate. Consider the black death in Europe during the middle ages, the Irish Potato famine, Ebola or the Spanish Influenza of 1918. These were real events that happened without humans even trying to inflict death on those people they hate. Very large monoculture farming and long distance food distribution is extremely vulnerable to attacks of this nature. Many small farms with a diverse genetic pool of plants/animals distributing food to local patrons would not easily transmit the dangerous problems that could be associated with an attack of this nature.

Unsustainable farming techniques combined with natural climate change can cause events like the Dust Bowl period of 1930-1936. This was a disaster caused by drought but it could have been mitigated by using the dryland farming techniques that were subsequently developed to address this problem. The Department of Agriculture should pay farmers to test experimental farming techniques that might address future potential problems that could be as significant as the dust bowl. This would benefit future generations in our country and be a more rational type of farm subsidy program.

Preparation for potential destructive events just makes sense to me especially when they have a significant probability of occurring. Farmers might as well make a profit from government money designed to mitigate disasters. Sticking our heads in the sand with our rear hanging out will not help us. The Amish will probably simply ignore most of these catastrophic events when they occur because their society is resilient and self sufficient being based on the small farm concept. The Amish are not dependent on our government for survival.

Our government should actively seek to replicate some elements of the Amish example for the purpose of american civilization survival in the event of disaster conditions occurring in our country. Small local farms are simply too useful in a pinch to be relinquished and thrown away on the ash heap of history. When the manure hits the fan someday it will be necessary to deal with it. Continued survival of our country is greatly enhanced by the existence of many small local family farms capable of producing food with minimal technological input.

Social Media Help

"Without counsel purposes are disappointed: but in the multitude of counsellors they are established."

Proverbs 15:22

The Bible is a website and app with many different standard translations of the Bible in English. The app will read the Bible to you. The creators of the website have probably never heard of my books and do not endorse them at all but I strongly recommend you take a look at this website/app. You can friend people on the website and communicate with them easily.

(https://my.bible.com/bible)

Glenn's Books on Amazon is where you can buy this book and other *Glenn's Books*. (http://amazon.com/author/glennsellnow)

My blog has a lot of accurate information that may help you or at least give you a chuckle if you need one.

(glennsellnow.wordpress.com)

Good News

"that if you confess with your mouth Jesus as Lord, and

believe in your heart that God raised him from the dead, you

will be saved;"

Romans 10:9, NIV

"And he said, The things which are impossible with men are possible with God."

Luke 18:27, NIV

Feedback,Reviews and

Testimonials

"Buy the truth, and sell it not; also wisdom, and instruction, and understanding."

Proverbs 23:23

Please leave feedback comments about this book at my website (glennsellnow.wordpress.com) or on amazon at at my author page amazon.com/author/glennsellnow. I am always looking for ways to modify and improve my books. Your comments would be greatly appreciated and help me with that endeavor. I may make periodic revisions to this book and future books under consideration based on your feedback.

If you have found this book useful or entertaining please leave a positive review at amazon.com/author/glennsellnow. You may also leave a testimonial on any subject at my blog glennsellnow.wordpress.com by using the contact form on the site or simply leaving a comment on any post.

This book was very easy to write. All I had to do was live my life and allow reality to happen. Just write it down and you have a book. I will be happy to sign your hard copy of my book if you buy one. You can contact me at my blog glennsellnow.wordpress.com.

God Bless you and thanks for reading my book!

www.ingramcontent.com/pod-product-compliance
Lightning Source LLC
Chambersburg PA
CBHW020604220526
45463CB00006B/2438